MORE
TRY THIS ONE

Edited by Thom Schultz

Illustrations by Alan Wilkes

IDEAS FOR
YOUTH GROUPS

P.O. Box 481
Loveland, Colorado

Selected from the regular feature "Try This One" in GROUP,
the youth ministry magazine.

TRY THIS ONE

Fifth Printing

Copyright © 1980 Thom Schultz Publications, Inc.

ISBN 0936-664-00-2

Library of Congress Catalog Card No. 80-80947

Printed in the United States of America

Contents

Introduction

Welcome to a zany collection of youth group ideas. All of these ideas have been contributed by youth group members and leaders from across the country.

In these pages you'll find crazy ideas, beautiful ideas, funny ideas, serious ideas, and a few very strange ideas. And you'll find some ideas to help your members grow closer to one another, and closer to God.

Have some fun reading through this collection. Then select a few ideas to try in your group. Since your group is unique, not all of the ideas will work in your group. Feel free to adapt, add to, or combine ideas to make them suitable for your group.

Be adventurous—try something really new.—*Thom Schultz*

Crowd breakers

shaving cream hairdos

Here's a hilarious gag for which you may want to have a camera handy.

Three guys sit in chairs, facing the audience. Three girls (one behind each guy) have full cans of shaving cream. At a signal, the girls empty their cans of shaving cream on top of the guys' heads, and then fashion "hairdos" out of the stuff. Set a five-minute time limit.

The audience then judges best, worst, etc.

Have towels on hand to clean up.—*Ron Wilburn, El Paso, Texas*

tp salesman

What you don't know can be pretty funny. And this activity promises lots of laughs.

Appoint a member of your group to be a "salesman." Pick someone who is usually good at making excuses, etc. Explain that the salesman must persuasively sell the group on the contents of a briefcase (or paper bag) without knowing what's inside. Send the salesman out of the room to ponder his sales pitch.

Now, show the rest of the group the contents of the briefcase—a roll of toilet paper.

Call back the salesman. He must now try to sell his "product" with convincing authority. Everyone in the room may now ask him one question about his product. The salesman must give a detailed answer.

As you can imagine, some of the answers are going to be hilarious.—*Carl Medford, Vancouver, British Columbia*

moo test

Here's a funny group gag about mooing.

Send four people out of the room. Bring back one of them and tell him that he must determine the loudest moo-er in the group. The entire group then moos on the count of three. Repeat two more times. Allow the person to identify the loudest moo-er. Tell him he's wrong and point to someone else (anybody) who was the "real" loudest moo-er. Tell him his wrong guess has earned him the duty of being the loudest moo-er for the next person.

Bring in the next person and repeat the procedure. Only, this time, on the third moo nobody moos except for the first person, who usually moos at the top of his lungs. (The rest of the audience must be clued in beforehand about the third moo.)

Do the same procedure with the other two people.—*Ron Wilburn, El Paso, Texas*

easy come—easy go

Here's a fun game that requires no skill.

Round up about 20 items to give away as prizes, such as stuffed animals, Cokes, water guns, Twinkies, etc. Arrange these items on a table in front of the group. Pass out pieces of paper and pencils and ask everyone to write down ten numbers between 1 and 75.

Now explain the rules: The leader will rapidly call out three numbers between 1 and 75. People who have one of these numbers on their sheets may run to the table, grab a prize, and return to their seats. This procedure is repeated until all prizes are claimed. Now, when numbers are called, people with winning numbers may run to a person who already has a prize and claim it for themselves. Each time new numbers are called, the prizes switch hands.

Whoever is holding the prizes on the last call gets to keep them.
—*Bob Brewer, Delmar, New York*

rubber band faces

Rubber bands can create funny faces. Here's how.

Put a large rubber band around the heads of several volunteers. Place each band so that it squashes the nose and folds over the ears. On a signal all contestants try to get the bands down around their necks. First one to do it wins.

One catch: they may not use their hands. They may only use facial expressions, walls, other people, etc.

This is a riot to watch.—*Ron Wilburn, El Paso, Texas*

musical pies

Like messy surprises? This one's for you.

Everyone stands in a circle. One or two whipped cream pies are passed in a clockwise direction while music is playing. When the music is stopped, the members left holding the pies may throw them at anyone in the circle (including the leaders).—*Rev. Gregory Bye, Dayton, Washington*

bong game

Here's a fast way to learn names.

Each person takes a name tag and writes his or her name and draws his or her favorite fruit.

Divide into groups of six to eight. Sit in a circle with one person in the middle, who is "It." "It" has a small section of newspaper rolled up. He or she begins by calling someone's favorite fruit. Then, that person responds by calling out his or her fruit and the fruit of another person in the circle.

The object: "It" tries to hit a person on the head (with the newspaper) before he or she can call out his or her own fruit and the fruit of another person. When "It" succeeds, the person who is caught then becomes "It."

After 10 minutes, play the game again—this time using the names from the name tags. People really learn names fast!—*Allen Dundek, Minneapolis, Minnesota*

hum that tune

Here's a musical ice breaker.

Count your members and give everyone a slip of paper with the name of a song on it. Use the same song for every four to ten slips of paper.

On the count of three, everyone begins humming his or her tune and tries to find others with the same tune.

This is a great way to get acquainted and to get divided into small groups for games or discussions.—*Gil Garcia, Menominee, Michigan*

egg blow

For this you'll need two people with strong lungs!

And you'll need a clear tube (about 3 feet x 2 inches) and one raw egg.

Break the egg into the tube, but make sure it doesn't come out the other end. The two volunteers then put the ends of the tube in their mouths. At the count of three, they blow.

The one with the weaker lungs gets a mouth full of raw egg.—*Jane Marasco, Hendersonville, Tennessee*

lemon squirt

Here's a game that will pucker out the participants and keep the spectators in gales of laughter.

Go to your local grocery store and buy a bunch of those plastic lemons that contain real lemon juice. Then give one lemon to every two people participating in the game.

One person must put the lemon in his or her mouth with the squirt end out. The other person stands close and puts his or her mouth up to squirter.

Then, on a signal, everybody begins squirting. The first couple to squirt all their juice wins the game.—*Brewster McLeod, Lexington, Kentucky*

cookie shiners

Here's an ice breaker particularly good for first meetings with a large group where everyone may not be acquainted.

Place a platter of extra large size, homemade cookies in the center or front of the room. Members in turn must address the group by giving as much pertinent information about themselves as they care to, but they must include at least one specific accomplishment or hobby about which they can brag. After this, each person takes a cookie and rubs it on his or her nose, chin, elbow or anywhere else.

Since no two people may rub or "shine" their cookies on the same place, not only is it amusing toward the last, but the group pays close attention to each speaker.—*Joan Moore, Denver, Colorado*

introducing...me

This idea was originally used at a coffeehouse my group sponsored which was attended by about 50 young people from four churches.

A short pencil and an ordinary 8 ½" x 11" sheet of notebook paper should be given to each person at the door. Have everyone print on his sheet of paper his name (first and last), and his favorite activity (hobby, occupation, pastime). Stress that one should be careful to list an activity that one will not be embarrassed to have made known publicly.

Everyone should attempt to introduce himself to everyone else, taking care to relate the exact information on his paper. The object is to memorize the names and favorite activities of as many people (outside of one's own group) as possible. Encourage the learning of additional information, also; it makes it easier to remember the required information. Besides, the underlying purpose of the game is to give everyone a chance to make new friends. After two persons have learned each other's names and favorite activities, they should sign each other's sheet of paper and move on to someone else.

It would be a good idea to set a certain time during the evening when introductions may be made. At the coffeehouse we gave, everyone sat attentively at card tables during performances. But intermissions looked like Chinese fire drills as everyone rushed about to introduce himself to someone new.

At some time during the evening everyone should enter the number of names and favorite activities he is confident he can remember on a chalkboard and write his initials beside his claim.

You might offer first, second, and third place doorprizes. Albums or tapes make good prizes, maybe a book, perhaps a poster. When you're ready to award the doorprizes, have those who entered a claim on the board recite their memorized names and favorite activities (having the corresponding people stand up), beginning with the highest claim. Remember, no one may include the names and activities of persons in his own group, lest those from larger groups be given an unfair advantage. Also, no claims may be changed once the recital of names and activities begins.

For each correct name *and* activity, one scores a full point. If one remembers the name but forgets the activity, or vice versa, one scores half a point. The top three scorers, of course, win the doorprizes.

And everybody wins a bunch of new friends.—*Tim Holland, Gulfport, Mississippi*

ducky-wucky

How well do you know the mystery voices in your group? Try this one to find out.

Everyone sits in a circle on chairs, with a blindfolded person in the middle. The person in the middle carries a pillow. He tries to find someone's lap. When he does, he puts the pillow on their lap and says, "ducky-wucky." The person he sat on must try to disguise his or her voice and say "ducky-wucky" back. The blindfolded person must then try to guess who it was. If he or she guesses right, then that person is "it."—*Bonnie Saltsburg, New Bloomfield, Pennsylvania*

name learner

Here's a fun and funny way to learn names in your group.

Form circles of eight to ten people facing inward. Choose one person as the starting point for each circle. This person begins by introducing himself using his first name only, preceded by a descriptive word beginning with the first letter of his first name. They can be as serious or as silly as each individual chooses. (Examples: diligent Dotty, jolly Jerry, brawny Bill, etc.)

Moving clockwise, the next person re-introduces all the persons before him and adds his name at the end until the person chosen as the starting point has to name all the people in his circle.

Example—Starting Person: "Hi, I'm bubbling Bonnie." Next Person: "Hi! This is bubbling Bonnie. I'm laughing Linda." Next Person: "Hi! That is bubbling Bonnie. This is laughing Linda. I'm fantastic Freddie."—*Dorothy Forman, Detroit, Michigan*

merry-go-round mixer

Here's a fun and interesting way to get acquainted in a group.

Form two circles, inner and outer, facing each other. Inner circle talks to outer circle with five statements, two minutes each. Shift to the right after each two-minute subject. Outer circles may ask questions but make no other comment. After five statements, the same process is repeated with the outer circle doing the talking. The leader will read the statements and call time.

Inner circle:
1. If I could visit any place in the world on vacation...
2. If I could smash one thing and one thing only...
3. If I had only one more day to live...
4. The time I feel most alone is...
5. The greatest force that has changed history...

Outer circle:
1. The greatest crime one person can commit against another...
2. The greatest discovery I'd like to make...
3. The greatest value in my life at the moment is...
4. The thing I fear the most is...
5. The thing that gives me the greatest satisfaction is...—*John H. Boller, San Diego, California*

no cottonballs

This is a fun game to watch.

Take two volunteers and sit them opposite each other at a table. You'll need some cottonballs, two spoons, and two bowls. Lay out the cottonballs and give the spoons to the volunteers to hold in their mouths. Tell them the object is to get as many cottonballs in the bowl while blindfolded. Now tie on the blindfolds. Catch: take away the cottonballs. This is hilarious!—*Rhonda Freeman, Morrilton, Arkansas*

co-op spelling

This mixer stresses cooperation (and a knack for spelling).

Pin a large card bearing a letter of the alphabet to each member's arm. And give each person a small card and a pencil.

The goal is for letters to get together and spell words. Once you've spelled a word, write the word on your card. Then separate and look for new words.

Award a prize to the person with the longest list of words. And you might award a special prize to the members involved in making the longest word. —*Ed Morris, Santa Maria, California*

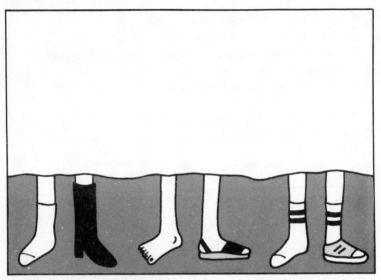

Cinderella shoe match

This is a fun crowd breaker and a zany scheme to divide your group into pairs for other games or activities.

As each girl arrives, ask her to remove her right shoe. (This in itself is rather unusual and should provoke curiosity right away.) After you've collected all the shoes, send the girls into another room. Then give each shoe to a boy to hold.

In the other room, have the girls step behind a sheet that is hanging from the ceiling. Only the girls' feet should show under the sheet curtain.

Then call in the boys and have them find their partner by matching the shoe they're holding with the shoe under the curtain. Or, to add some difficulty, have the girls remove the other shoe so the guys have to try to fit the shoes, Cinderella-style. —*Julie Brandon, Bryan, Ohio*

spoofers

Did you ever want to prove your power of spoof? Here's your chance.

A word nobody knows is chosen from the dictionary. Everybody writes a believable definition for it. The one with the dictionary writes, in his own words, the real definition. The definitions are gathered up, read aloud and each person votes for the most likely one.

You get one point for voting for the real definition. Each vote for a phony definition gives the creator of it one point. Pass the dictionary.
—Bruce Filson, Montreal, Quebec

bubble gum blast

Your group can have a blast with do-it-yourself bubble gum.

For $2 you can buy a package of bubble gum mix that will make almost a pound of chewy fun. Bring your group together for an evening of bubble gum-making. It's really easy, and great fun. The more you stretch it, the better the chewing.

Then, once your gum is made, have contests. Award prizes for the biggest bubble, loudest bubble pop, the largest number of bubbles inside each other, etc.

You may order bubble gum mix from some confectionery and candy wholesalers. —Doug Newhouse, Florence, Kentucky

secret party

This plan is simple, secret and fun.

The leader picks a home for a party to be held after a youth meeting or an evening worship service. The home is usually that of one of the young people. The leader contacts the parents, who in turn prepare some "goodies" for the party. Meanwhile, the location is kept a secret by the leader and the parents. (If possible, the kids of the host parents should not even find out.)

Then after the meeting, the leader loads up his kids for the hunt. The group is then led on a "wild goose chase." By this time, the group will be making guesses as to where the destination really is. When you arrive, some may have guessed the spot, but most will be surprised. Do this once a month. My group looks forward to it.
—Rhett Payne, St. Louis, Missouri

pass the peas

Here is an unusual way to build togetherness in your group and have fun doing it.

Sitting in a circle, each group member is required to give his name and then make a distinctive statement about himself. (Examples: "I can do four one-handed push-ups," or "I can recite the Pledge of Allegiance while standing on my head.")

The person to the right of person #1 can do one of two things. Either she can doubt #1 or she can believe #1. If she doubts #1, then #1 must show that he can do the feat he claimed. If #1 can do it, then person #2 is required to eat a spoonful of cold peas (from a can). If #1 cannot do it, he is caught in his bluff, and he must eat the peas.

If person #2 chooses to believe #1, then #2 must attempt the feat —so as to prove that person #1 is not the only person in the world who can do it. If #2 accomplishes the feat, then #1 has to eat the spoonful of peas. If #2 cannot, then she must eat the peas.

The game continues around the circle. Now #2 makes a claim, and person #3 must be the judge.

This game often uncovers some great hidden talents in the group. —*Paul Borthwick, Lexington, Massachusetts*

action announcements

Announcement time in meetings is usually when everybody is talking and nobody is listening, right? Well, we have attempted to change all that, and it has been successful.

Prior to the service, I briefly write out the pertinent information regarding the announcements on separate pieces of paper and fold them up. Then, I read through the announcements and decide which method of making the announcements would be most effective, and label it such. Next, I write the number of participants that will be required to make the announcement on the outside of the folded paper.

Then at the beginning of our service, I ask for volunteers to help me. (I don't mention what or how they will be helping.) As I glance through the announcements, I choose the youth that I feel would do the best job at each of the various methods of announcing. Usually I try to involve six to ten youth in this announcement time, and the response is terrific! These individuals leave the room for about five minutes of preparation before they have to present their announcements to the group. I send one or two youth sponsors out of the room with them to help them as they prepare. While these youth are out of the room, the rest of the group is singing or doing a crowd breaker, etc. After about five minutes, I call them in, one announcement at a time and they perform it or demonstrate it to the group.

The great thing about it is that it requires audience participation, and we know that people learn and retain longer those things in which they are an active participant.

Some of the various methods of demonstrating or performing the announcements that we have found to be effective are: charades, pantomime, poetry (making the announcement rhyme), news reporting, alternating words (two individuals do the announcement by each reading every other word).

An example of how the announcement would look as it is given to the performer: "Pantomime—1 person, CAR WASH: this Saturday at the church from 10-4."

It's exciting and fun! Your group will love it! But, don't wear it out—use it maybe once a month or decide what is best for your group.—*Darrel M. Johnsen, Auburn, Washington*

knee sit

Here's a good crowd breaker—and a good exercise in group unity.

Everyone gets in a circle and turns to the left, facing the back of the next person. Then, on the count of three, everyone sits down on the knees of the person behind them, still holding to hips of the person ahead of them.

If everyone sits in unison, and no one falls off, you should be able to stay in that position for some time, quite comfortably.—*Linda Sharp, South Weymouth, Massachusetts*

balloon shavers

Suspense surrounds this crowd breaker.

You'll need balloons, razors and shaving or whipped cream.

Break your group into boy-girl couples. Each guy blows up a balloon and sits in a chair facing the girl. She then spreads the shaving

cream or whipped cream (it tastes a little better) onto the balloon while the guy holds it in his mouth.

Now comes the fun part. The girl then attempts to shave the cream from the balloon with the razor. The first couple to remove all the cream from the balloon without popping it wins.

If you use shaving cream, remember to close your eyes.—*Dave Silvey, Alexandria, Pennsylvania*

"what" game

Here's a crazy game that uses your members' creativity.

Each person is handed four scraps of paper and a pen, and he or she writes a question beginning with "what" on each of the four blank papers. The papers are collected and redistributed.

Now each person writes an answer to a "what" question on the back of each of the four pieces of paper *without* looking at the questions. (Don't peek!)

The papers are again collected and redistributed. Now each person reads aloud the four papers—questions and then answers.

Amazing results! You'll all be sure someone peeked! Now try it with "who," "where," etc.—*Bruce Filson, Quebec, Canada*

marshmallow drop

Do certain members of your group start complaining right at the end of the meeting about their stomachs growling? If so, they should be perfect subjects for this fun game.

Choose three "hungries" from the group. Also select three "droppers." Spread lots of newspapers on the floor. Have the "hungries" lie on their backs on the papers.

Give each "dropper" a small paper cup of melted chocolate and six marshmallows. On the count of three, the "droppers" stand over the "hungries" and dip the marshmallows in the chocolate and drop the gooey gobs into their partners' mouths.

The team with the most marshmallows eaten is the winner.—*Roxy Bishop, Harper, Kansas*

long yarn

Need to get acquainted? Here's a good idea to try when you have a lot of new faces at a meeting or other activity.

Pass around a ball of yarn and a pair of scissors. Allow everyone to cut a piece. It may be from one to twelve inches long.

Now, everyone should sit in a circle. Here's the catch: for every time each person winds the string around his finger, he must give some fact of his life. Get ready for some long yarns.—*Michael Imperiale, Highstown, New Jersey*

Games

guys' beauty contest

Begin by auctioning off all the boys, one at a time, to the highest bidding girl (or group of girls who are pooling their resources).

Once all the boys have been purchased, the girls may take them to different rooms for an hour to dress them (as girls!), fix their make-up, hair, etc., and train them to do something for the talent portion of the beauty contest.

When ready bring everybody back together and begin the contest. Remember that the purchased "slave" is his "master's" representative in the beauty contest. If he wins, his master wins.

Now bring in your judges—your youth pastor and some friends recruited ahead of time, unbeknownst to your young people. The judges should rate each contestant in several categories—best dressed, most poised, best talent, etc.

This is an event full of laughs and fun.—*Phil E. Quinn, Nashville, Tennessee*

chain relay

Here is a different twist on a relay. There are two main differences between this and an ordinary relay. First, instead of team members performing individually, they are all joined at the hands (and secured with masking tape), and must do everything together. Second, instead of performing tasks in a given order, the different tasks are at stations around the room, and teams may try them in any order they wish (except for the final task).

Teams of three or more people join hands to form a line. The leader sticks the joined hands together by wrapping them with masking tape. This is to ensure that the group stays together.

There must be at least two more tasks than teams. Some suggested tasks are:

1. Fold a paper airplane.
2. Cut out a shape from a piece of paper.
3. Roll up a newspaper and put a rubber band around it.
4. Untie and tie the shoe of the middle person.

5. Feed each member of the group a marshmallow.

6. Blow up and tie off a balloon.

Use tasks that require two hands.

FINAL TASK: The whole team must do a somersault together without breaking its grip.

There are only two rules to this game:

1. The final task must be done last.

2. If a grip is broken, the whole team must return to the leader to have the grip re-taped before continuing.

This game can be used to illustrate the idea of the body, community, and working together. And it's a whole lot of fun besides.—*Jim Steele, Lake Oswego, Oregon*

sock grab

This is a great game for a retreat or large group.

Tape off a large circle on the floor, large enough to seat the whole group. Remove your shoes before sitting in the circle. (You must wear socks to participate.) On a "go" signal, try to collect as many socks as you can—any way you can get them! You're out of the game (and the circle) if both your socks are taken or if any part of your body goes outside the circle. The last person in the circle wins.—*Jane Marasco, Hendersonville, Tennessee*

cross corners

Here's a game that everyone can enjoy.

Divide your group into four smaller groups and put each group in a corner of a large room or gymnasium. Then a game commander shouts that all groups are to proceed to their opposite corners. The first group to have all its members reach the opposite corner wins that round.

Now here's the catch. The game commander decides how the groups are to proceed across the room—walk, run, walk backward, tip-toe, crawl backward, slither, etc.

The collisions in the center of the room are hilarious.—*Allen Dundek, Minneapolis, Minnesota*

egg roulette

Here's a game filled with suspense and lots of laughs for the group.

You'll need two volunteers and six eggs (five hard-boiled and one raw). Be sure none of the eggs has any cracks or markings that would give it away as being hard-boiled. Volunteers cannot handle or inspect the eggs before choosing them.

One volunteer begins by picking one egg and cracking it over the other person's head. Then the other volunteer does the same. This continues until someone gets the raw egg.—*Ron Wilburn, El Paso, Texas*

CB hide 'n' seek

Now that almost everyone has a CB radio, this is a game that your group can enjoy.

Divide the group into teams in as many CB-equipped cars as you have. Each team will be given the opportunity to hide, and seek.

Team A is given five minutes to drive anywhere in the area and park the car. After five minutes, all other teams begin searching for Team A. Every two minutes Team A must give a clue as to its location. For example, during one game, we hid at a Gulf station. Our clue was, "We're in a GOOD place," referring to that company's "Good Gulf" ads.

When a team finds the hiders, it wins five points. If a team remains hidden for 30 minutes, it wins 10 points and ends that round of the game.—*Tony Thomas, Harrison, Ohio*

Bible treasure hunt

This game is especially suited for a youth retreat, or some other setting in which there is plenty of room. It is best played outdoors.

Before the game, select a Bible verse, one which is fairly well-known to your group, but one which no one will think of immediately. Write each word of the verse on a separate piece of paper, and hide the pieces of paper at various locations around the play area. Compose a set of clues, in duplicate, which will direct the players to each one of the hidden words. Unlike an ordinary treasure hunt, the clues do not form a chain; each clue directs the players to a separate hidden word.

Now divide your group into two teams. Give each team a complete set of clues. The two teams (which each have an identical set of clues) will compete to find the single set of hidden words. Most likely, each team will end up with roughly half of the hidden words of the Bible verse. Once each team finds as many of the words as it can, it gathers at a previously designated location to try to unscramble the Bible verse.

Now the real fun begins. In all likelihood, neither team will have found enough of the words to figure out the verse. At this point, the teams are permitted to bargain with one another, trading one word for another until one of the teams wins by figuring out the Bible verse.

The key to winning this game is organization and cooperation. The teams are competing with each other for the same set of hidden words; therefore, the team which first sits down and brainstorms about the clues, then delegates certain team members to go out and retrieve the words, will do much better than the team which immediately runs out helter-skelter. A wide range of abilities is essential—not just speed in running, but also skill in problem-solving, verbal ability, and familiarity with the Bible. Thus, all team members can feel that they played a part.—*Carlos Wilton, Princeton, New Jersey*

banana relay

This game is as fun to watch as it is to play.

Get enough bananas to have one for every two people in the group, plus a few extras. Divide into two or more equal teams (you may have one person go twice if you're lacking a person). Two people will have one banana. They peel the banana and place it between them with opposite ends in each other's mouths. Then they run together around a chair placed about ten feet away and back to their team. Then the next two people peel their banana, and so on.

Each pair scores three points for completing their run without breaking their banana, one point for making the run with a broken banana. The first team to have all its pairs complete their runs gets five extra points.

Assign a scorekeeper to each team. The team with the most points wins.

wild transportation

The Young Life club of Kaufman, Texas, challenged young people at the local high school to a "gettin' there is all the fun" contest. Participants were required to come to the meeting at the leader's house by the strangest means of transportation they could think of.

One guy rode a unicycle to the meeting carrying another guy on his shoulders who was toting a sign reading "*YOUNG LIFE OR BUST!*" Another pair of guys rowed across the lake behind the leader's house in a bathtub rigged to pontoons with a Goodyear bicycle flag fluttering on the mast. As they reached the shore the plug fell out. Two pin-striped "convicts" were chased to the house by a Texas Highway Patrol car with siren, flashing lights, and the patrolman yelling "one last chance to surrender, one last chance to surrender!" through his megaphone.

Others used more conventional means of transportation, such as hoppity-hop balls, old-fashioned wheelchairs, pogo sticks, skates, stilts, tricycles, and souped-up playpens complete with steering wheel, headlights, horn, and siren.

Seventy young people showed up for the meeting at which there was a promised free spaghetti dinner for the most unusual stunt. There were a lot of spaghetti dinners awarded that night.

do-nothing machines

Though no one in our group had heard of Rube Goldberg, we had a lot of fun for free with this one.

Gather materials such as broom handles, boxes, rope, marbles,

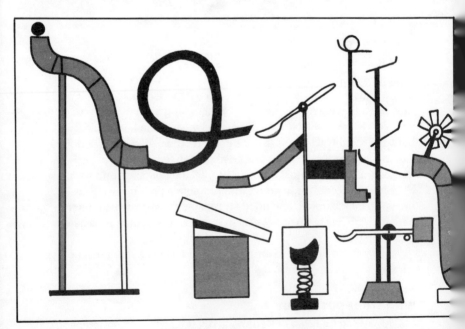

cardboard tubes, potato chip canisters, volleyball-type balls, old books, etc., and lots of masking tape.

Set a time limit of at least 45 minutes and divide into small groups of two or three. Each group (with common access to the provided materials) creates, constructs, and operates their own Rube Goldberg do-nothing machine. Whoever creates the machine that, once set into motion, keeps going the longest without human help, is the winner.—*Jim Flachsbart, Albany, Oregon*

nose squirters

Here's a game with a little skill and a lot of laughs.

Make two rows of people, facing one another, about four feet apart. The people in the first line are to be given a squirt of shaving cream on their noses. And each person in the second row gets a squirt gun.

On a given signal, those with the squirt guns try to shoot the shaving cream off the noses of those in front of them. You win by squirting clean your partner's nose.—*Ronda Freeman, Morrilton, Arkansas*

jousters

Here's an exciting waterfront game. Needed are two canoes, paddles, two jousting poles and two people in each canoe.

The jousting poles are about 10 feet long and are padded on one end by tying on towels or old clothes.

One person paddles from the back of each canoe. As the canoes are lined up facing each other, about 20 feet apart, the two jousters stand in the front of their canoes. As they meet, the goal is to see who can knock the other into the water first.—*Erik Bjorn, Prince George, British Columbia*

giant "clue" game

Everybody's played that table game, "Clue," right? Well, it's great fun as a life-size game, too.

Use the homes of your members as the possible places of the "murder." Your parents are the subjects.

The object of the game (as in the smaller version) is to find out who the murderer is, which weapon was used, and where it took place. Clues are found by going to the homes and asking the parents questions. At each home, you may only ask one question. It may be a "yes or no" question about one suspect, one weapon, or one place.

The parents at each house will have certain answers (having been given only so many cards bearing the name of a suspect, weapon or place).

You may go to any home as many times as you wish, but not to the same place twice in a row.

Divide your teams by carload and the first team back with the correct answer is the winner.—*Erin Bjorn, Prince George, B.C., Canada*

sardines

This is a fun game for small to medium size groups.

You'll need a large indoor area. Everyone gathers in one room or area. Then one person goes and hides. The rest of the group waits a few minutes then scatters to try to find the hider.

Here's the catch—when someone finds the hider, he must join the hider in the hiding place. This continues on until the last seeker finds the rest of the group wadded up inside the hiding place. This is really fun when the hider chooses a small, cramped place to hide.—*Gregg Almquist, South Weymouth, Massachusetts*

amoeba race

This game's a riot, but it takes real team work.

Divide your group into two teams. Tie a long rope around each team, bunching everybody together tightly. Set up a course for the two teams to run, perhaps out 50 feet, around a box, over an obstacle, and back again.

Then, it's "on your mark, get set, go!" The teams won't move very fast, and may even collide and crumble, but it's great fun.

To guard against crunched toes, all team members should remove their shoes.

thread and spoon

Here is a game that makes you dependent upon one another and helps to promote working together.

Divide into two groups (more if your group is really large) with the same number of males on each team, and the same number of females on each team. Teams should line up boy, girl, boy, girl, etc.

Each team will need a spool of thread with a spoon tied to the end of the thread.

The first person on each team must drop the spoon down through his clothes. The next person must bring the spoon up through her clothes, while the person continues to feed thread from the spool, under his clothes to the next person. This pattern must be followed to the end of the line, up one person and down the next.

When the spoon reaches the end of the line, it must be fed back to the first person the same way it came. The first team to complete this task without breaking the thread is the winner.—*Dan Sewell, Omaha, Nebraska*

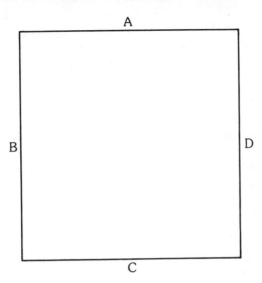

A

B   D

C

crazy soccer

For variety and excitement, we invented some adaptations to the game of soccer.

Use the basic soccer rules and field, or whatever will suit you best. Divide into four teams, such as freshmen, sophomores, juniors and seniors. The freshmen (using A as their goal) play against the sophomores (using C as their goal). At the same time, the juniors play the seniors, with the juniors using D and the seniors using B.

This will cause havoc as the teams collide and try to avoid each other. Though the teams will bump, they may kick only the ball assigned to their two teams.

Then have the winners of each game challenge each other while losers play one another.

Then for more variety still, combine the freshmen and seniors into one team and the juniors and the sophomores into another team. These two teams now play each other—using all four goals. The first team defends goals A and C while the other team defends B and D. You may use two balls instead of one.

For the final game, you may have the girls challenge the guys. But each of the guys must tie a 30-inch rope between his ankles.—*Bill Rudge, Sharon, Pennsylvania*

watermelon keep away

When we go to the beach or lake we always take several watermelons. The kids go wild over them.

Everyone goes out until the water is about chest high. We divide into three or four teams and play "keep away" by passing the watermelon under water. Sometimes it pops up and flies through the air.

27

After everyone has had their fun playing "keep away," we cut the melons and have a watermelon feast.—*Ron Bodager, Metairie, Louisiana*

ice blocking

This crazy idea is called "ice blocking."

Buy one or two 25-pound blocks of ice. Go to a grassy hill with a good slope. Bring a towel to place on the block of ice. Then sit on the ice and ride to the bottom of the hill. The first few times it will be slow, but later on it is great. You can sit, lie, or stand on the ice with one or two people.

Then, if everyone buys a block of ice, you can have races.

The ice block lasts longer than you might think, depending on how hot it is outside. Normally it lasts up to 1½ hours.—*Ron Bodager, Metairie, Louisiana*

water balloon volleyball

Need a refreshing new way to play volleyball? Use water balloons instead of a volleyball!

Prepare a batch of water balloons. Then proceed to play volleyball in the regular way, but using a balloon for a ball. When a balloon bursts, it's a point for the team on the other side of the net. No spiking allowed. But you may catch the balloon and toss it over the net, rather than swatting it.

For added fun and strategy, fill some balloons more than others. —*Rachel Rae Johnston, Haviland, Kansas*

cotton nose blowers

Here's a game that's fun to play and funny to watch.

Each member is given the chance to carry cotton balls across a line and drop them. The person who has carried the greatest number of cotton balls across the line in 30 seconds is the winner.

Sound easy? Well, there's a catch. The cotton balls may be carried only on the nose. Here's how it works. Each member smears some Vaseline on his/her nose. On hands and knees, members poke their noses into the cotton balls on the floor. When they get a cotton ball to stick they crawl a couple of feet to the line and disengage the cotton by blowing. Hands may be used for nothing but crawling.

The game may be played with individual competitors or with relays.—*Sue Herman, Grand Rapids, Michigan*

Nerf elimination

Here's a fun game that really gets people down on their knees—

and backs and stomachs.

The game is launched when the "commander" throws the balls (three or four Nerf balls) into the air. The balls are then "shot" at each other. When you are first "wounded" you must either play on your knees or bottom. The second time you are wounded you must play on your back or stomach. (During this time you should still be "shooting.") With the third wound you're "dead" and must sit out until the next "battle."

The game shows that in war, nobody wins. —*Kari Beth Fisher, Austin, Minnesota*

forward and backward

Here's a fun game. Everyone should sit in chairs in a circle. Then a leader gives instructions such as: "If you have on any green, move forward one chair." "If you didn't brush your teeth today, move back

three chairs." "If you talk in your sleep, move back one chair."

If someone is in the chair you move to, just sit on his/her lap. You can stack people three or four high.

The first person to make it all the way around the circle wins. —*Ronald Fritts, Findlay, Ohio*

egg drop

Test the engineering ability in your group. Organize an egg drop contest.

The object is to design an egg carrier that will protect the contents from breaking.

Divide your group into teams of four. Give each team a raw egg, a roll of masking tape and several pages from a newspaper. The team then must create a carrier for the egg that will withstand a sudden shock. Establish a time limit (perhaps 20 minutes) for completion.

Then bring all teams to a drop-off point. This could be a balcony, a roof or atop a ladder. Lay out a plastic cloth down below. Each team then drops its egg on an "X" marked on the plastic cloth. If an egg survives the drop, its team is a winner.

This is a lot of fun. And you may be surprised at some of the wild crash cases created by the teams.—*Virginia Myers, Greeley, Colorado*

electricity

"Electricity" is a game everyone can enjoy. To start, everyone sits or stands in a circle and joins hands. One person stands in the center of the circle.

Someone starts the "current" going by squeezing the hand of one of his neighbors. And this person then sends it on around in the same way.

You may not switch directions once the "current" is started.

The person in the center has to find out who has the "current" and call out the "carrier's" name. If he's right, those two switch places and the "current" is started around again. The person in the center cannot watch the person who starts the "current."—*Lima United Methodist Youth Fellowship, Howe, Indiana*

scripture sounds

Here's a scavenger hunt for sounds.

Divide your group into teams. Provide each team a tape recorder (make sure batteries are good), microphone, blank tape and transportation. Each team is to find, record in sequence and bring back the sounds that correlate with your scripture study within the time limit (suggest 30-45 minutes).

Here's an example for 1 Corinthians 13 and 14:

1) 1 Corinthians 13:1—a clanging cymbal or gong (any unusual noise would do.)

2) 1 Corinthians 13:4-11—ask three individuals to define "love": a. a small child; b. someone "going steady" or engaged; c. someone married more than 25 years.

3) 1 Corinthians 14:7-8—someone playing a musical instrument like a flute, trumpet or harp.

4) 1 Corinthians 14:9—your entire team competing to repeat tongue twisters.

When the groups return, play back each recording to judge the best. Then correlate the significance of the sounds with the scriptures.

Verse 10 of Chapter 14 tells us that no sound is without significance.—*Herb McMillian, Bradenton, Florida*

Polaroid scavengers

Here's a great team activity with lots of laughs.

Divide your group into carloads. Give each car a Polaroid camera, film and flash bulbs. The object of the game is to get pictures of specified things, with points awarded for each photo. Here are some

sample photo subjects and their game points:
- picture of you with a policeman, holding your hands up (900 points)
- McDonald's employees with french fries sticking out of their mouths (200 points)
- all members of your team on a goal post (500 points)
- a boy in women's clothing (800 points)
- your team on a fire truck (700 points)
- people in a telephone booth (150 points)

The list goes on with about 25 items. And since you have only 8 or 10 pictures, you try to get the ones with the most points.

Allow two hours for the hunt.

The carload with the most points wins, and the other cars treat the winners to pizza.

The best part of this game is looking at the goofy pictures in the end. We pasted our photos on a board so everyone could see them.
—*Connie Relos, Buffalo Grove, Illinois*

artist's folly

Here's a fun and funny game.

Your leader prepares two lists of items, such as: phone, shoe, apple, tunnel, hot dog, trampoline, salad, etc. Come up with 20 items,

10 on each list.

Divide your group into two teams. Then one person from each team goes to the leader. The leader whispers the first item on list #1 to the representative from team #1, and whispers the first item on list #2 to the person from team #2. Then the team representatives run back to their teams with a pencil and paper and attempt to draw their items. They may not say anything or write any words. Only artwork is allowed.

Each team looks on and tries to guess what is being drawn. When the team finally guesses, the person who guessed correctly runs to the leader to hear the second item on the list.

This continues until one team wins by guessing all 10 items first.
—Chris Yost, Bladensburg, Maryland

ankle bone connected to the...

Find out how quick and coordinated your members are with this one.

All girls stand in a circle. Then all the guys form a circle around them. The inner and outer circles must contain an equal number of people, so you may need to make some adjustments.

The girls begin walking clockwise while the guys walk counter-clockwise. The leader then interrupts by calling out two parts of the body. For instance, he might call out, "Wrist to nose!" or "Knee to elbow!" At that moment, both circles stop. Whomever you stop next to is your partner with whom you must assume the designated position.

Eliminate the slowest couple each round. Award a prize to the survivors.—Lori Smith, Macungie, Pennsylvania

you've come a long way, baby

Gather home movies and slides of some of your members when they were babies. At your next meeting, show three or four sets of pictures and have the group try to guess who the "stars" are on the screen. If you wish, you may award prizes to the right guesses or to the member who makes the most right guesses.—Bob White, Apoka, Florida

looks like rain

Divide the group into two teams. Each team gets an overcoat, an umbrella, and a hat (the sillier the better). On the signal "go," the first person in line puts on the hat and overcoat, opens the umbrella over his head and shouts, "It looks like rain." They pass the items on to the next person who does the same thing. The first team through wins.

Variation: For those too superstitious to open up an umbrella inside, they may choose to put the tip of the umbrella on the floor, and while holding the handle, dance in a circle around it singing,"I'm singing in the rain."—*William Grady Roe, Austin, Texas*

anything goes

Have an "Almost Anything Goes" tournament, inviting other churches to participate as teams. We held ours at a farm. Some of the events we featured were a wheelbarrow obstacle course where the driver was blindfolded and the person sitting on the wheelbarrow gave directions; a catapult made by jumping on a board, sending a playground ball into the air (the one hitting closest to a target wins); a baking contest where in relay teams one person puts mud on a pie plate and tosses it to someone else who puts some "Decorations" on top, then tosses it to someone else who stacks them(most pies made in a minute wins); an obstacle course made with tires, boxes and things to jump over; a balloon toss. Total team points determine the winner.—*Paul Warder, Monroe, Wisconsin*

no teeth

Here's one of those "you only lose when you laugh" games.

Have your group sit in a circle. From this point forward, you may not show your teeth. To speak, you pull your lips inward around your teeth to hide them.

One member starts by asking the person next to him,"Is Mrs. Mumble home?" The person responds, "I don't know—I'll have to ask my neighbor." This keeps going around the circle. When someone's teeth show due to laughter, he's out.

Smiling is permitted provided the teeth don't show.

When asking or answering, contorting the facial muscles may be used to try to "crack up" the person next to you.

When the group narrows to the strong ones, it's good to rearrange the sitting order to weed out any "closet laughers."—*John Fisher, Beltsville, Maryland*

match book treasure hunt

This is a fun treasure hunt involving restaurants in your community.

Make up riddles about the various eateries in your area. Here's an example: "If an Italian and a Hawaiian married, and moved from Italy to Hawaii, their combined nationalities would demand that they live in a ......" (Answer: Pizza Hut.)

Divide your group into carload teams. Give each carload a copy of the riddles. The teams must solve the riddles, drive to the restaurants, and obtain from each restaurant a match book that advertizes that particular place.

Each restaurant is assigned a point value according to the distance from your starting point. Set a time limit and have more restaurants than teams could possibly reach in the allotted time.

Award a prize to the winning team.—*Kurt Picker, Houston, Texas*

hot air football

You've heard of air hockey. Well, this is hot air football.

Cover a long table with butcher paper or newsprint and mark off a football field. Divide into two teams. Seat your teams around the table as shown in the diagram. Use a ping-pong ball.

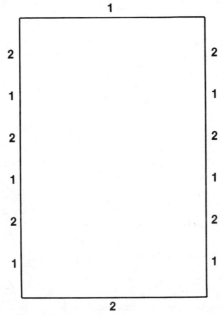

The object is to score by *blowing* the ball down the field and across the goal. Any number of penalties, plays, etc., can be created.

Only one player may defend the end zone.

Players cannot use hands, head or any part of the body. You may only *blow* the ball.

NOTE: This game is not recommended following hot dogs and onions.—*Mr. and Mrs. S. Perry Holleman, High Point, North Carolina*

gloved gum game

For this crazy game you'll need paper bags, gum and gloves.

Divide your group into two or more teams. Give each team a pair of gloves and a paper bag containing sticks of gum.

On a "go" signal, the first person on each team takes the pair of gloves, puts them on, grabs a piece of gum from the bag and unwraps it using only his or her hands and teeth. Then he or she begins chewing the gum and passes the gloves and bag to the next person.

The first team to finish is the winner.—*Lois Silvey, Alexandria, Pennsylvania*

finger maze

To play this game you must first create your own maze. Obtain a large panel of cardboard from a cardboard box, such as a refrigerator carton, and cut a variety of narrow (about 2 inches wide) paths with a knife or razor blade. There should be many detours and dead ends to make the game more fun and interesting.

Players are not allowed to see the maze before playing the game.

Players are blindfolded and led to the maze one at a time. Place the player's index finger at the starting point on the maze. Time how long it takes for each player to reach the finish. Players are not allowed to use their free hands to explore possible paths.

The player with the shortest time is the winner.

If you allow each member to create a maze, you could also award a prize to the member who created the most difficult maze.—*Eric Preibisus, San Diego, California*

bigger and better hunt

Here's a scavenger hunt based on gaining weight.

Divide into groups of 4 or 6 and give each group a small item, such as a piece of string, a button or a cottonball. Then each team goes door to door in your neighborhood, exchanging its item for something bigger and better. For example, if you start with a button, you might exchange it for a jar, then a shoe box, then an old chair, etc.

Set a time limit of two hours.

The team returning with the biggest and best item wins.—*Rebecca Bolthouse, Traverse City, Michigan*

pumpkin pelvis push

This is a weird game for your Halloween get-together.

Divide the group into teams of four. Give each team a pumpkin of the same approximate size. For each team, place a chair 20 feet away. If you have four teams, use four chairs.

The object is for each team representative to push his pumpkin around his team's chair and back to the next player on his team. The first team to have all four of its players finish is the winner.

The catch is this: the players may use only their pelvises to push the pumpkins while doing the crab walk sideways.

For added excitement and chaos, have two or three teams going around the same chair.—*Mark Kaat, Sheboygan, Wisconsin*

team tree decorators

This idea is guaranteed to add excitement to your Christmas parties. Advertise a Christmas Tree Decorating Contest (with prizes), but add that this one will be different than ever before.

Divide the group into teams. Each team is given a bag of decorations (one flashlight, a roll of toilet paper, a box of tinsel, and a few plastic flowers). Members are also allowed to use their scarves, hats, coats and gloves.

The unique part of this contest is the "tree." Rather than a typical Christmas tree, each team *is* the tree. Teams are given five minutes to plan, and then given the command to make themselves into a human pyramid, decorating themselves as they go. After a set time (three to five minutes) the trees are judged and awarded their prizes.

Failure to stay in position while the judging is taking place results in disqualification.—*Paul Borthwick, Lexington, Massachusetts*

winter William Tell

Here's a game of skill and laughs.

Divide into teams. Each team selects one member to be the "target." The target stands 20 feet away from the team with a stocking cap perched lightly on his head, and his back to the group.

At the whistle, the entire team launches snowball after snowball at the target in an effort to knock off his cap. The team with the fastest time in knocking off the cap is the winner. (Other hits to the target's body do not count for extra points!)—*Stan W. Kesler, New Haven, Indiana*

Group growth goodies

kidnap breakfast

This is primarily a fun activity but can do a lot for building spirit in a youth group.

The advisor awakes about 5:30 on a Saturday morning and uses a station wagon or large van to go to the homes of the youth group members to pick them up. The young people have no idea what's up.

The driver goes to the first home and wakes up the young person there and both return to the car. Having been so rudely awakened, the young person is eager to do the same to the next person on the route. This is done until all the members of the group are in the van.

The group then returns to the home of the advisor where his wife or other advisor has been making pancakes, bacon, etc., for breakfast.

Each member of the group must come dressed in whatever he or she sleeps in (or with a bathrobe on).

One very important note: the advisor must notify the parents of the youth group so that they will not be surprised when the doorbell rings early in the morning.

Our group has enjoyed this so much that they ask when we will do it again (but we don't tell them as it would spoil the surprise).—*Paul E. Wedlock, Groton, Massachusetts*

cookie decorators

A simple sugar cookie recipe is needed plus some imagination to put together an experience that provides a built-in snack and sharing session for your group.

Each person is given a small amount of cookie dough and asked to make one or two cookies that represent something important in his/her life. Food coloring and "extras" (such as decorating candies) may be added to make the cookies come to life. It doesn't take long to bake the cookies in the oven (10-15 minutes).

Once all are finished, put them on display and ask each member of the group to tell why he made the kind of cookie he did. After the sharing of ideas, share the cookies!—*David Shaheen, Silver Spring, Maryland*

decision-making

Everyone makes decisions daily. Obviously, some are more important than others. Some are so important that they require thought, study, investigation and prayer before a decision is made. These decisions may include buying a car, getting married, changing jobs, etc. Some decisions, like whether to drink tomato juice or orange juice for breakfast require little thought. They are "automatic," and we make many of that type of decision every day. It is important to know which decisions require deliberation; different people will have different answers.

On the form below are 10 typical decisions. On the lines below these, list 10 more decisions that you have made during the last week or month. Try to include decisions from each of the following categories: personal and social decisions; health and safety decisions; educational and career decisions; moral, ethical and spiritual decisions; and common, everyday decisions.

Now, on the lines labeled "Rank," write in a number from 0 to 5, using this scale:

0—not generally perceived as being under your control; decision is usually made by others.
1—automatic or routine; never think about it before deciding.
2—occasionally think about it before deciding.
3—think about it but don't study it or investigate it.
4—study and think about it a little; ask others about it a little; ask others about it before deciding; perhaps pray about it.
5—study and think about it a lot; ask questions; read about it before deciding; pray about it.

DECISION	RANK
1. To get up in the morning	....
2. What to eat and when	....
3. To tell the truth	....
4. To criticize a friend behind his back	....
5. To change jobs	....
6. To stop at stop signs	....
7. To drive beyond the speed limit	....
8. To believe in God	....
9. What classes to take	....

10. To do homework ....
11. ....
12. ....
13. ....
14. ....
15. ....
16. ....
17. ....
18. ....
19. ....
20. ....

After everyone has filled in the form, discuss your decision-making processes. Where do you agree and disagree? How should we establish our decision-making process? Should we consult God before every decision? Should decisions about our faith in God be automatic, or should they be carefully studied?—*John Hall Boller, Jr., San Diego, California*

love room

We all have a hard time showing love sometimes. And occasionally cliques and small, tight groups of friends really hurt others by their messages of rejection. Here's a group exercise that may help.

You'll need two separate rooms with four or five people in each room. The rest of the group is kept in another room.

One by one, the leader sends a person into the first room for a few minutes. Here the four or five people have been told ahead of time to ignore the newcomer who has been instructed to introduce himself and to try to join the little group.

After the newcomer has been in that room a short time, the leader takes him to the next room. Again he introduces himself. But here the four or five people enthusiastically greet him, smile and hug him. After he recovers from all the love, he stays in that room to greet the others in the same way.

After everyone has experienced the cold room and the love room, have a discussion on how each person felt in each room. Relate the experiences to everyday life.—*Larry Schultz, Milton, Wisconsin*

mystery ride

Everybody loves surprises. Announce a mystery bus ride. Only the leaders will know your destination.

For our mystery nights, we all load a bus and use a rotation seating system. The people next to the window stay seated. Every three minutes a whistle is blown and the people sitting on the aisle rotate clockwise. This is a great way to meet the people in the group.

The destination should be an hour or two away, and could include a meal with the price of the bus ride. You could go to an amusement park, a zoo, a tour of some industrial plant, or other destination. It's a real thrill to find out where you paid to go.—*Connie Relos, Buffalo Grove, Illinois*

pillow talk

Do the members of your group feel free to express themselves? If not, maybe your problem is that the only mode of self-expression available at your group meetings is the spoken word. And we all know that words just don't always get the full message across. Maybe what your group needs is the simple acquirement of some pillows.

Yes, I said pillows. Stock your meeting place with an abundance of multicolored, interestingly shaped, soft pillows and you'll give the less oral types just what they need to fill in the gaps which their oratory always seems to leave.

How? Like this. At my group's last weekly meeting, one member asked another how the other felt about something she had said. Colleen, the one asked, was at a loss for words. Fortunately there was a basketball sized pillow handy, which, without a moment's hesitation, Colleen seized and flung across the room where it struck the wall. Actually, she'd been aiming at the person who'd asked the question. Then Colleen explained, "It made me kind of mad." Colleen had expressed herself. And we got the message.

But pillows also help express other feelings besides anger. Does something make you happy? Toss a pillow into the air—hurray! Did something embarrass you? Bury your face in a pillow until the subject changes.

Pillows also have more practical purposes. Is the furniture in your meeting place uncomfortable? A pillow in the right place could fix that. Are there times when the group wants to be closer? Don't move the furniture closer together—form a circle of pillows on the floor. And for those of you who, like us, operate on a tight budget, good news! Pillows can be made inexpensively. There's no need to buy them ready-made. Make the pillows as a group project.

So if you want a new mode of expression which can make your group meetings more comfortable or more intimate, try pillows.—*Tim Hollard, Long Beach, Mississippi*

gift list

Here's an activity to help your group recognize and value the gifts God has given you.

Hand out blank sheets of paper, and have each participant number down the page from one to ten. List the gifts you have—the things you do well. Then look over your list and place a star beside the gifts you really enjoy using.

Now, gather in groups of four to share your lists. In your groups, focus on one person at a time, helping that person identify the gifts and abilities he or she might have missed.

Spend a few moments considering your abilities and how you might use them to help others.

Now divide your foursome into pairs. Choose one or two of your gifts and help one another think of ways these gifts can be of value to others.

Reassemble into the total group and think about the list you made. Was it difficult to identify your gifts? Were you surprised to discover you could list so many? Or so few?

Share what you learned during the experience.—*John H. Boller, Jr., San Diego, California*

progressive variations

Every youth group in the whole world has had a progressive supper—a supper served in three or four courses, each at a different location (usually in homes). The group progresses from appetizer to salad to main course to dessert. They are loads of fun.

Well, here are some different twists to the traditional progressive supper:

1. Travel by bicycle or any other kind of wheels (roller skates, skateboards, etc.) to locations. Keep mileage down.

2. Serve courses outdoors, picnic style.

3. Eat each course in a different restaurant: appetizer at a health food store (they offer all kinds of juices and snacks), salad at a pizza place, main course at McDonald's, dessert at Baskin-Robbins.

4. Use four different rooms in the church. Decorate them to represent four different foreign mission areas your church suggests. Serve the native foods of the areas. Brief presentations (slides, panels, talks) can explain the ministry you're seeking to provide in each area.

5. American ethnic meals can be arranged in homes, or at the church. At each serving, the situation of each ethnic group can be dramatized...soul food with information on ghetto life; Polish food with a look at Polack jokes; Indian food with a discussion of the plight of America's natives; etc. In each case the group can deal with misinformation and generalization regarding each ethnic group.

6. Scripture progressive supper, in which a passage of scripture and a group experience is set up at each course, as follows:

a) Appetizer: group forms a circle on the lawn of the host's home. Read John 13:1-16. Leader explains why foot washing was a custom in a time of sandals and dirt roads and how Jesus used this task to teach his disciples about servanthood. A comparable custom in our time is the washing of hands before a meal...usually done alone, but this time the group members will wash one another's hands. All you need are a basin of water, a wet towel and a dry towel. While the group is doing this in silence, the scripture could be read again or soft group singing could be going on.

b) Salad: group forms a circle on the lawn of host's home. Read Luke 14:16-24 regarding The Great Banquet. Leader points out that Jesus has invited us to a great feast, and a lot of us still give excuses for not giving ourselves to him.

c) Main course: group circles up as before. Read Matthew 25:31-46, followed by information on world hunger. Luke 12:45 is quoted. Blessing is said for the entire progressive supper.

d) Dessert: group circles as before. Read scripture where Jesus tells Peter, "If you love me, feed my sheep"—John 21:4-17, followed by a modern day parable about the man who was given a glimpse of hell and heaven. Taken to hell, he saw people sitting at a lavish banquet, but all were in great grief due to the fact that long utensils had been strapped to their arms so that their elbows could not bend. Therefore, they could not feed themselves. Then he was taken to heaven where he saw the same lavish banquet and the same utensils strapped to the people. But these people were happy, full, singing and joyous...for they were feeding the persons seated across from them.

Then the leader asked group members to pair off and to feed each other dessert, after which the benediction is given.—*D. Ray Wiggins, Brentwood, Tennessee*

regressive dinner

The process is the same as a progressive dinner...you go to different homes for each course of the meal. The hitch here is that you do everything in reverse—start with the dessert, then move to the main course, salad, appetizer.

If you really want to have fun, have everybody wear their clothes backwards.—*C. Daniel Jessee, Richmond, Virginia*

traveling hoagie

Here's a new twist on the old progressive dinner idea. Instead of eating a different course at each stop along the way, you progressively build a hoagie (submarine sandwich).

Plan to travel to each of your members' homes. At the first stop you'll get the bread and slice it. Additions at later homes could include ham, cheese, onions, oil and vinegar, lettuce, tomatoes, etc.

Hoagie "accessories" could also be added—chips, salads, soft drinks and dessert.

At your last stop, you'll finally have a feast!

One word of caution: be sure to find drivers who won't mind driving cars that'll smell like hoagies for a week.—*Glenn Megill and Sam Miller, Farmingdale, New Jersey*

blind trust

This exercise is especially effective in building group unity and trust.

Everyone stands together in a large circle in an area free from any obstructions. One member of the group stands in the center and be-

comes the "walker." The walker holds his arms straight out, with eyes closed tight. The walker then spins in place two or three times and then starts walking straight ahead without opening his eyes.

When the walker approaches one of the members standing in the circle, that member then moves forward, grasps an arm, and then swings the walker around and lets him go back in toward the center of the circle. The walker keeps moving in that direction, blind to any orientation, until a member at the opposite end of the circle grasps an arm and swings him back again. The process repeats itself time and again for a couple of minutes and then a new walker is chosen.

The objective of this exercise is to keep the blind walker out of harm's way by leading him always back into the center. When the group becomes particularly familiar with this exercise, a second walker might be sent in at the same time. With two walkers, however, the outer circle members have to be especially careful where they point the walkers, lest they run into each other and hurt themselves. This is where the element of trust plays an important role. The walker must display confidence in the group by blindly submitting himself to their rule. The group in turn, must be careful not to betray that trust and allow the walker to get hurt.

Each member of the group should have a chance to be the walker. Just a few minutes of this exercise is bound to bring almost any new group closer together.—*Michael Hofferber, Boise, Idaho*

cookie,cookie

This is a game that helps to build trust and confidence between members of a group. It is best played out-of-doors, in a park or a wide field, free from any dangerous ditches or streets.

The group divides up into pairs. One member is blindfolded and placed at the mercy of his or her partner, or guide.

The guide is to lead the blindfolded group member on a tour of wherever the game is being played.

The blindfolded member is forbidden to remove the blindfold until the tour is ended.

The guide is forbidden to touch the blindfolded member in any way (unless, of course, to keep the member from harm) and he can say nothing more than "cookie, cookie."

The guide then leads the blindfolded member by calling out, "cookie, cookie." This is the only communication that takes place between them. Differences in the tone, pitch, speed, and direction of the voice alone will guide the tour. After a time the members should switch roles and partners to give everyone a chance to guide and be guided. —*Michael Hofferber, Boise, Idaho*

forgiveness test

This activity is designed to help participants examine their attitudes about forgiveness in relation to the behavior of others.

Write the following situations on a chalkboard:

—Mrs. Jones steals food for her hungry family.

—Billy steals 50 cents from his father's wallet.

—15-year old Rita shoplifts with a group of friends for kicks.

—Bartender Louie goes looting during a riot in the inner city.

—Judy requisitions small articles from the place where she works and takes them home for her personal use.

—Jimmy snatches a purse from an old lady who has just cashed her welfare check.

—Mary steals money from a wealthy home where she is baby-sitting.

—Nancy pads her expense account.

—Mike steals drugs to support his habit.

—Once again Perry steals your time—promises to meet you for lunch and doesn't show up.

Now, choose the three persons you are most willing to forgive. And choose three you are least willing to forgive.

Then, find a partner and talk about the following: why you made the choices you did; the person on the chalkboard who bothers you the most; how God might see some of these situations. —*John H. Boller, Jr., San Diego, California*

soap carving

Soap carving is easy, simple and a good way to share important symbols in your life.

All you need for each person is a bath-sized cake of soap and a paring knife. Carve your cake of soap into a symbol (no matter how simple) of what is important to you right now.

Then, after a set time period, each person explains his or her sculpture and shares why this symbol is important.

You may end the experience by giving your symbol to someone else, as a tangible way of sharing what you value most.—*David Shaheen, Silver Spring, Maryland*

hunger game

The complexities of world hunger can be explored in this fun game.

Divide into teams of six to eight persons. Each member should choose a prepared name tag: "FARMER," "GRAIN DEALER," "GOVERNMENT OFFICIAL," "RUSSIAN MERCHANT," "STARVING ETHIOPIAN," "CONSUMER AND TAXPAYER," and "CHURCH LEADER." Drop the "RUSSIAN MERCHANT" for teams of six; add another "FARMER" for eight.

Each member will need an equal amount of play money, except for "ETHIOPIAN" and "FARMER" who will receive no money.

The "FARMER" should be given a small bag of popcorn, each kernel representing 100,000 bushels of grain.

You may wheel and deal with each other in your team however you wish. And the "GOVERNMENT OFFICIAL" may levy taxes at any time (the "RUSSIAN" and "CHURCH LEADER" are tax-exempt).

Everyone should know that score will be taken at the end of 20 minutes. At that time, each member should rate his/her satisfaction with the proceedings on a scale of 1-10 (with 10 being ecstasy). Write your rating on your name tag. Post the tags by teams and total. Highest "wins."

Discuss the experience.—*William H. Levering, Muskogee, Oklahoma*

hunger service

We had a super youth-led worship service based on hunger in the world.

The pews in the church were divided into geographical areas of the world—South America, North America, Asia, Africa and Europe. We reserved three rows for Europe, five for North America, 18 for Asia, etc. The congregation was then seated according to each area's population. We put 15 people in each European row, five in each North American row, etc. The congregation was able to feel how crowded or spacious their world area was.

During the service, a youth represented each world area, talking back and forth with the other world representatives. "Why don't the people over in Asia get themselves a job?" asked one representative. "Well, why don't you people in North America share more of your resources?" asked another. We had some very touching speeches.

Other young people sang songs related to hunger. And we showed related films and filmstrips.

For communion, each world area was given bread and wine in the ratios of how much food (per person) their area really has today. Asia was given only a half loaf of bread to share among everyone. North America was given four loaves. We had hoped the people with surpluses would share with those in need. It was interesting to watch the sharing start to happen. Two small children were the first to share.
—*Laura Rushton, Grosse Pointe Woods, Michigan*

photo revue

Here's a great way to build group spirit and have a few laughs. Assign someone in your group to be the group photographer. This person then takes pictures (slides) of all your group activities over a three-month period.

Then, every three months have a big slide show. Keep the show moving at a good pace, and be sure to include plenty of funny shots.

This activity promotes your program by showing different activities. And it gives a responsible job to your youth photographer. Plus, it's a fun time that your members will really look forward to.—*Bill Blue, Flint, Michigan*

snapshot browser

We keep a teen club photo album in which snapshots of our participation in various activities form a pictorial history of our group.

When someone is interested in joining our group, a look through our album is an ideal way to show what we're all about.—*Dorothy Forman, Detroit, Michigan*

construction site art

Many large construction companies often have to build fences or walls of wood around their sites that are in high traffic areas. Did you know that their public relations offices will often buy paint and brushes if young people will do the designing and painting?

We decided to try this and we invited kids from 10 churches to participate. More than 200 kids showed up. The mayor came by and gave trophies to the best panels. We had radio, TV and newspaper coverage and made a great day of it.

Here's how to set it up. After your group decides to look into the project, contact the construction company public relations depart-

ment. Convince the P.R. people to buy the paint and brushes, etc., if you'll supply the people. Then, members should submit sketches on a given theme, such as "Springtime in Atlanta" or "What the World Needs Now Is Love."

When Paint Day comes, distribute the various colors of paint in paper cups to all your artists. Call the news media. Arrange for the mayor or other official to judge the colorful panels and award prizes.

And you don't need a group full of professional artists. Those members with some artistic talent can be given the job of sketching the large murals—and everyone else simply fills in the blanks with their paints. Beautiful!—*Ben Mathes, Decatur, Georgia*

people collages

This is a good experience to discover how others see us.

Each member of the group writes his or her name on a slip of paper and places it in a hat. The hat is then passed around and everyone chooses a name other than his own.

Then look through old magazines and newspapers and cut out any words or pictures that describe the personality of your chosen person. Then create a collage of your person by pasting onto a sheet of construction paper all the pieces you've cut out. Since this is a positive experience, everyone should be discouraged from portraying negative sides of people's personalities.

After everyone is finished, display the posters and see if the group can guess who is described by each collage. Then have each poster creator explain his or her creation.—*Dave Silvey, Alexandria, Pennsylvania*

light and love feast

This is a fine idea to use to close a retreat or special gathering.

First, give everyone a candle. The leader shares several scriptures about Jesus being "the light of the world." A large candle burns near a picture of Christ. The leader then lights his or her candle from the large candle and shares one special word (such as love or peace) and what that word means to him/her. The leader then spreads the light by lighting someone else's candle. That person then shares a special word and its meaning and lights another person's candle. This continues until everyone's candle is lit.

Now invite observations about the experience.

You're now ready for the love feast. Gather everyone around a campfire or fireplace, if possible. Everyone is asked to find and read a scripture that contains the word "love." You might give a few hints: 1 Corinthians, 1 John 3 and 4, Romans 12, and John 13-15.

After it seems that the last scripture has been read, everyone should get up and stand beside someone and tell that person why you love him or her. This may be done one at a time or all at once. Some people may wish to express love to more than one person.

This is a meaningful experience that could be repeated on an annual basis.—*Ron Bodager, Metairie, Louisiana*

living water

This is a fun and meaningful learning experience.

Ask everyone to bring any kind of container that holds a liquid. Any size or shape is okay, but should include a lid. Each person then lists the ways he or she uses water in a week's time.

Then, everyone hikes to an unknown destination selected by a leader. Here everyone fills his or her container from a creek, well or other water source.

Now someone should read the scripture of Jesus and "living water" (John 4:5-14). Using a large poster, list the ways we are all different (like the containers), but can still have "living water" within us. Then list the ways "living water" can be used through us.

The containers of water could then be used at home during the following week to water plants as a reminder of physical service. —*Charlotte Randall, Titusville, Pennsylvania*

love raffle

Here's a raffle where nobody is the loser.

For your next gathering of lots of kids, pass out name tags that each have a number. Then have your raffle, drawing several numbers from a hat.

The prize? It's "the love of the brethren!" Have the winners come to the front of the room. Then encourage everyone to come and express their love to the winners—hugs, handshakes, hellos, etc.

We've used this several times. Without fail, the winners really feel special and never forget the experience.

If you wish, you can "rig" the winning numbers to be sure to include those shy, depressed or unknown people who really *need* the experience.—*Gil Garcia, Menominee, Michigan*

church live-in

Need unity in your group? Try living at the church for a week.

Our group lived at the church for one week during the school year. We set goals for the week, and everybody had to sign a commitment paper agreeing to live at the church all week.

We moved in on a Sunday evening after church.

Each morning we ate breakfast together and had a short devotional. After school was a time of fun and doing the jobs around the

A·WILKES

church. Each member took turns preparing meals, washing dishes, sweeping the floor and cleaning the restrooms.

Each evening we had a time of sharing and singing. On Monday evening we had a special speaker who talked on unity. A musical group came in on Wednesday evening. On Friday evening, we invited the parents for a potluck supper, games and singing.

Super personal relationships and group unity were really developed over this week.—*Sherry Mast, Goshen, Indiana*

family feud

Here's a fun idea we used to climax a four-week seminar on parent-teen relationships.

We did a take-off on the "Family Feud" television game show. We invited all the young people and their parents. Two families were chosen as contestant teams. The winning family received free dinners at a local restaurant.

For our "audience survey group," we used a class from a local school, with the cooperation of the teacher. Those kids completed a written survey that gave us our "popular opinion" answers for the game.

Here are some of the questions that we used: What is your father's favorite food? What is your mother's favorite treat? (One wise guy answered, "My father.") What do you like most about your parents? (Surprisingly, "strictness" was the number one answer here.)

The game is a lot of fun, and it helps to communicate some parent-teen understanding.—*Ray Cooper, Beckley, West Virginia*

prayer advocates

Here's a warm way to share God's love with others in your group.

Form a circle for group prayer. Any person in the group can ask the group for prayers for another person in the group by standing behind that person and placing his or her hands on the shoulders of that person. At that time, anyone in the group may offer a silent or spoken prayer for the designated person. The advocate closes the prayers with an "amen" or a spoken prayer.

balloon confessions

We often overlook the Christian practice of confession of sins. Here's a meaningful experience to bring meaning to the act of confession and forgiveness.

You'll need one helium balloon for each person in your group. And you'll need a batch of felt tip markers. Each person writes on the balloon a sin that he or she wishes to confess.

Then the group goes outside and offers a prayer for forgiveness. And each person silently talks to God about his or her sins and then releases the balloon, symbolic of God's forgiveness.—*Paul Taylor, Dallas, Texas*

nail soup

Have everyone bring something to put into a pot to make "nail soup" (stew). It may be meat, vegetables, mushrooms, etc. Show the movie, "The Nail." After the film, have your dinner of "nail soup" and talk about the movie; also tie it in with the Body of Christ passages from the Bible (Romans 12:4-8), explaining that just as we each brought something for nail soup and made a delicious meal, so we are part of the Body of Christ, making something very special when put together. You may want to conclude with Gaithers' "Something Beautiful" from their "Live" album.—*Paul Warder, Monroe, Wisconsin*

custom devotionals

It's hard for a lot of us to set aside a devotional time each day. And, good devotional guides are hard to find. So, we solved the problem by writing our own. The kids really get into it and share the homemade guides with their friends. The friends are interested because the booklets are written by people they know. Each member selects a favorite Bible verse and then writes what it means to him. The youth pastor then writes a thought and challenge for the day.

Here's a sample page from our booklet:

"For God has said, 'I will never, never fail you nor forsake you.' That is why we can say without any doubt or fear,'The Lord is my Helper and I am not afraid of anything that mere men can do to me.' "—Hebrews 13:5b-6.

"This verse has meant a lot to me since I moved to Arcadia because I had to change schools right in the middle of the year. For some reason, I'm afraid of school and I, like most others, despise going back after vacation.

"But Jesus has helped me to meet a lot of Christian friends at school and I'm learning that school is nothing to be afraid of.

"There are so many verses that talk about not being afraid and everyone can help you, too. Just think of what this verse says about fear."

THOUGHT: "Is there anything that scares you about school and friends? What about your future? What scares you today? Trust Him right now to give you peace and to help you deal with things that get you afraid."—*Mike Slater, Hacienda Heights, California*

thinking of God

Attributing human characteristics to God is called anthropomorphism. God has used this often in the Old Testament when references were made to his hands, voice, feelings, etc. The following are value clarification strategies which will help us understand how we think of God today.

Place an "x" on the line which represents your thinking on the issue.

1. Using human years, how old do you think God would be?
1 yr. —————————————————————— 100 yrs.
2. How do you think God would dress today?
Mod ————————————————————Very formal
3. In your mind, God's mood with you is mostly...
Critical ————————————————————Accepting
4. How involved is God is the affairs of people today?
Passive————————————————————Active
5. If God would speak to you today, what would be the tone of his voice?
Very soft————————————————————Very forceful
6. God's work load in your mind would be...
Very busy ————————————————————Very casual

For the following, circle your answer.
7. If you had something to discuss with God, would you have to make an appointment with him?   YES/NO
8. Would you go to God or would he come to you?   GO/COME
9. Where would you meet him?   HIS OFFICE/OUTSIDE IN A PARK
10. How much time would be involved?   ALL THE TIME YOU NEEDED/ALL THE TIME HE HAD

After everyone has answered all the questions, allow time for voluntary sharing of answers, and discussion.—*John H. Boller, Jr., San Diego, California*

secret friends

Paul wrote in 1 Thessalonians 3:12, "...abound in love, one toward another." Elton John said the same thing just recently in his release, "Shower the people you love with love, show them how you really feel." This basic Christian concept is timeless yet so often we neglect to emphasize it.

There are many practical applications of this basic biblical theme that can be used in your youth group. Here's one:

Each member should put his name and address on a piece of paper and return it to the leader. Then explore the vital role of loving one another as a part of Christian growth. Discover Matthew 22:39, John 13:35, John 15:12 and 1 Thessalonians 3:12.

Now each member should draw a name from those put in the hat. During the following week each member should:

1. Write the person whose name you drew and tell him about the one quality in his life that you admire.

2. Include in this letter your favorite Bible verse or one that you have found particularly helpful.

3. And, pray daily for the person whose name you drew.

At your next meeting, share what this experience has meant to you. And, if you wish, draw names again...and continue to draw new names every week.—*Mary Thomas, Fayetteville, Tennessee*

it's the pits

"It's the Pits" is a whole evening of activities.

We started the evening with a "pit pass." We divided the group

into equal teams (six to ten on a team). Each team was given a Nerf ball. Then on the starting signal each member of the team passed the ball from armpit to armpit without the assistance of hands. If the ball is dropped or touched by a team member's hand, the team started over again. The first team to pass the ball successfully to each member and then back is the winner.

"Pit food" was next on the list of activities. We gathered as many different types of pitted food as we could find—cherries, plums, peaches, prunes, olives, apricots, etc. This was a race of who could eat the fastest. Between each eating event, the eater sent a runner to the closest restroom (for a pit stop) to bring back one square of toilet paper in which to place the pits.

The evening's talk centered around the pits referred to in the Bible (such as Proverbs 28:10) and how in our Christian walk the pit is "for the pits."—*Rev. Joel Williams, Citrus Heights, California*

the body

Read (or study) 1 Corinthians 12:12-26 to the group. Take a few minutes to discuss Paul's vision of Christians in community as the body of Christ. As a body, all members affect and support the others—if the head aches, the whole body suffers, if the eyes are closed the whole body stumbles, if the feet hurt the body won't get so

far.

Pass out pieces of paper and have each person write down the part of the body he or she thinks he or she represents, and why. For example, Joe is the smile, because he keeps us happy; Amy is the hand, because she works hard, etc. Then have everyone share their "part of the body." (This works well as a get-acquainted exercise, too.)

Celebrate the diversity and the interdependence of the parts with a song, or a prayer together, to affirm Christ's presence in your group. —Diane Luton, Mt. Berry, Georgia

feet washing

Most Christians are very good about observing the symbolic rituals of communion and baptism, but how many of them have ever been involved in a feet washing service? Christ said in John 13: 14-16 to "do as I have done" when he spoke of washing the disciples' feet. Symbols are very meaningful to young people, and the feet washing service is a very powerful and positive symbol.

Before the service, all members should thoroughly understand the meaning of feet washing. This can best be done by constructing an entire youth worship service around the event. Emphasis should be placed on what the act meant at the time of Christ, the need for having our feet washed (our feet get "dirty" during our Christian "walk"), and what it means to wash someone else's feet (servant attitude, to show love, following the example of Christ). It should also be understood that resistance to having one's feet washed shows a lack of trust (showing our imperfections) and an inability to accept love and help from another person (note Peter's reaction and the Jews' reply in verse 8).

If properly prepared, the service can carry a great deal of significance and impact. Divide into groups of six to eight, seated on the floor in circles. Place one chair in the center of each circle with a basin of water and several towels nearby. Begin by having one person in each group stand and select another group member by quietly taking his hand and seating him in the chair. The footwasher should remove the person's shoes and socks and then quietly wash and dry both feet.

The person who has had his/her feet washed then selects another member of the group. This continues until everyone's feet have been washed.

It should be noted that for many people the initial reaction to the idea of washing someone else's feet is humorous as well as distasteful. However, given the right preparation and encouragement this service can be both meaningful and revealing to your group.—Richard A. Nixon, Long Beach, California

spirit cards

We chose Galatians 5:22 and 23 for a brief study and the focus of a nine-week exercise. For this exercise, each member of our group was given a stack of nine 3" x 5" cards and a felt marker. Everyone was instructed to print one of the fruits of the spirit (as found in passage) on each of the nine cards. We were to break up and find a place where we could be alone and pray, asking God to guide our *judgment*.

We were then instructed to spread our cards out in front of us and to choose the fruit of the spirit that we thought was best developed in our own personalities. We took that card and placed it face up in front of us. We then picked the card that stood for what we believed was the second best developed fruit in our lives...and so on, until the end. The result was a stack of cards that, from the bottom to the top, contained the fruits of the spirit, in order, from the best to the least developed in our personal lives...a spiritual profile.

Each member was instructed to take his cards home and put them in a place where they would be seen several times a day. The cultivation of the fruit written on the top card was our assignment for the week.

Now, each week as we come together for our youth activity, a part of our program is devoted to a session in which our members break up into groups of 4 or 5. Each member of the group identifies his top card and rates his spiritual progress for the week. Each member offers encouragement to the others. The top card is removed and placed on the bottom of the stack. At this point, each identifies his new top card and that becomes his assignment for the next week. The members share how we hope to produce the newly assigned fruit of the spirit.

Our kids are really excited about this program. The very first question that is asked when we meet is, "What's your top card?"...and then, "How are you doing?"

At least two words of caution: first, no one should be permitted to believe that this exercise will result in spiritual perfection. No one is going to master one of the fruits of the spirit in the space of a week. This is only an awakening. We will be working on the fruits of the spirit for the rest of our lives. Second, everyone should be helped to see that we cannot produce these virtues by our own efforts alone. For the fruits of the spirit are just that...the fruit of God's Spirit, dwelling in the Christian's life.—*Lee Bracey, Warsaw, Indiana*

tutor service

Homework? Everyone needs help with that! A youth group in Texas formed a tutoring service for younger members of the church.

The group met one Saturday to plan the project. All members chose a subject they liked. They decided to work with elementary school students, because the homework would be easier for them to decipher. A local high school counselor talked to the group about tutoring methods. After a general discussion, the counselor talked about the special problems of tutoring each school subject the mem-

bers had chosen.

The group leader then wrote each of the member's names with the subject he or she had chosen on index cards, so parents could sign their child's name under the subject heading of their, or the child's choice.

The group agreed to hold the tutoring session from 3 to 5 p.m. each Thursday in the church annex. Members were asked to donate one Thursday (at least) each month. There were enough members in the group to assure that each of the main subjects would be represented each week.

The project was then announced in the church bulletin the following Sunday. Parents signed up after the service at a special booth and agreed to donate a dollar for each session to help fund future youth group projects. Parents also agreed to be responsible for dropping their children at the annex for their tutoring sessions and picking them up at 5 p.m.

The project was a great success, a service that was greatly needed and one that could benefit the members of the church. The children reported that their grades improved. Even the tutors said their school work had improved, since each lesson was a basic review of their earlier education. Both parents and school officials praised the project. The pastor saw the project as a service that would also serve to unify the church and its members as they worked together to help the youngest members.—*Sharon Saine, Little Rock, Arkansas*

Psalm 1, illustrated

Making a slide presentation from Psalm 1 is an excellent learning project for a youth group.

Begin the project by having a lesson or series of lessons studying the Psalm. Pick out and list all the "picture" words and phrases, such as:

"walk in the counsel of the wicked"
"stand in the path of sinners"
"tree firmly planted by streams of water"
......and so on.

Next, go out into the community and/or congregation and take a series of 35mm slides to illustrate the various phrases. For some phrases you might want to take a series of shots.

Then put together a slide presentation. This could take the form of a dramatic reading of the Psalm while the slides are being shown. If

some of your members are talented musically, they could put Psalm 1 to music and it could be sung in coordination with the slides.

Finally, present the slide show to the congregation during a worship service or other church function.—*Jim Gullett, Napa, California*

consensus seeking

Sometimes it's difficult to maintain a good discussion. One or two people or the leader often end up doing most of the talking. One way to combat this problem and to encourage maximum participation is through consensus seeking.

Consensus seeking can be used in either large or small groups, but is more effective with groups of 20 or fewer. No lengthy preparations are needed. Five sheets of paper are the essentials. Each sheet should be lettered in advance with one of the following: STRONGLY AGREE, AGREE, NEUTRAL, DISAGREE, STRONGLY DIS-AGREE. The sheets are then scattered over the floor.

The leader or a member makes a statement to which the group reacts by going to stand on or by the sheet with which they most closely agree. After everyone is in place, each member states his or her reasons for standing on a particular sheet.

After listening to each reason, members of opposing views try to persuade members of other opinions to come over to their side by varying and amending the original statement. When a member hears a statement that changes his or her stand, he or she moves to another sheet that more easily reflects this change. This process continues until all or nearly all of the group is standing by one sign.

Another way of utilizing this method is to have members hold up the signs instead of placing them on the floor. Members then go and stand in front of the sign that best expresses their opinions.

Although consensus seeking is useful in sparking discussions, it is not limited to this function. This is also an exciting way to involve your group in planning group activities. Instead of the leader throwing out a statement for group reaction, the members vote on individual suggestions as a starting point. All opinions get aired and the group is able to make use of any expertise in the group. This process takes longer than traditional planning methods, but the final decision is acceptable, at least in part, to all.

Consensus seeking is not a compromise or a majority vote, but a dynamic method of involving the total group in the decision making process.—*Ernestine Weaver, Florence, South Carolina*

nightcap

Plan a breakfast that begins at midnight. Invite people to come as they would to breakfast—pajamas, rollers in their hair, shaving cream on their faces, hair messed up, nightcap on, slippers on, toothbrush in hand, etc. Cook breakfast. Games can be flap-jack flipping, egg walk, shaving contest, hair fixing contests (guys fix girls' hair and vice versa). Skits could include "Early Morning News Show" with fictitious events involving kids in the group. Polaroid snapshots of people as they arrive add a special touch to the goings on. Post these pics on your bulletin board. All-night activities can include rap sessions, films, or even a housecleaning of the youth room, repainting, etc.—Bernard Johnson, Rockford, Illinois

talk circles

Want to improve your group's communication skills? Try this method and discuss the results.

Divide into groups of ten or twelve. Five or six members of each group form a small "talk" circle. The remaining members of your group surround them in an outside circle. The small "talk" group takes a controversial news topic or values question such as: Should the Equal Rights Amendment be passed? Or, should euthanasia be legalized? The members of the talk group are to openly discuss the question for ten minutes. Within that time they are to try to come to a group agreement on their answer to the question. The members of the outside group are not to participate in the discussion. Their role is to observe how well the talkers are communicating.

After ten minutes, have both groups discuss how well the talkers listened and responded to one another. Were the outside group members able to keep silent? What can you do to improve your listening?

Repeat the experience by choosing new talkers and/or a new topic.—S. J. Marinella, Mesa, Arizona

how are you?

How sincere are we when we greet one another? "How are you?" "Fine." Do we really mean it? Here's a group activity to explore this everyday phenomenon.

Station one of your members or leaders at the door as your group is arriving for a meeting. As people enter, the welcomer should say, "Hi, how are you?" Then, the welcomer or an assistant should write the response of each person on a 3 x 5 card. Now tape the card on the member.

When everyone has arrived, split the group according to responses. All those with cards reading "OKAY" will make one group. Those with cards reading "FINE" will make another group, and so on. Now each group is instructed to creatively design a skit on the meaning of "Hello, how are you, good-bye."

Present the skits and discuss.

Conclude with each member going to other members and *meaningfully* giving a verbal or non-verbal good-bye.—*Bob Cross, Flossmoor, Illinois*

Christmas in July

Most nursing homes receive group visits at Christmas and Easter, but rarely are they remembered during the rest of the year. With this knowledge, our youth group set out to surprise the patients of a local convalescent center for the Fourth of July holiday.

We made 150 red, white and blue tray favors—fluted snack cups wrapped in tissue paper and gathered at the top with a ribbon bow. Each one contained a religious medal and free samples of cologne

for the men and perfume for the women.

The social director and a few of the residents sent thank-you notes assuring us that our surprise was "like a cool, refreshing breeze during the long hot summer."—*Dorothy Forman, Detroit, Michigan*

Palm Sunday fair

While searching for a new way to learn about Lent and the events of Holy Week, we hit upon the idea of a Lent Event that we call a Palm Sunday Fair.

We spent the Sunday class periods from Ash Wednesday to Palm Sunday preparing for the event. We prepared collages depicting the words "crucifixion" and "resurrection" today, and displayed the collages along with cinquain poetry about Lent written by our members—to publicize the coming event to the congregation.

We then prepared games that would teach others about Lent and Holy Week.

Grades 3 to 8 were invited to join us on Palm Sunday during their regular church school hour to participate in the fair. Adults and younger children of the congregation joined the group during the fellowship hour after the class.

Teaching games included a bingo-type game highlighting scripture passages associated with the events of Lent and Holy Week; a board game that lit up when the correct answer was given to questions about the symbols for Holy Week; and a picture game in which the pictures had to be put in chronological order to show the order of events during Holy Week. The picture game utilized the line drawings from *Good News for Modern Man* which had been projected onto a wall with an opaque projector and redrawn by our members.

Poster boards were hung from the ceiling. Each poster board represented an important day during Lent from Ash Wednesday to Easter Sunday. Details about a particular day were spelled out on the poster boards so that the younger children who had not participated in the ongoing study could get answers to their questions.

Films on Lent from the American Bible Society were shown, and John and Mary Harrell's filmstrip and recording of "Christ Is Risen" were utilized.

A food booth served foods of the Holy Land which we had researched.

Our members served as facilitators during the fair, helping the younger children play the games, running projectors, serving food, and keeping things running smoothly.

The Palm Sunday Fair was a success from every point of view. We learned a great deal while preparing for the fair, and the children and adults learned by coming to the fair.—*Monica A. Brown, Potomac, Maryland*

graduates' banquet

Near the time of graduation, all members of the senior class are invited to a dinner in their honor in our parish hall. The parents are invited, too. The dinner is a potluck affair provided by the parents and members of the junior class in the parish.

This affair is not one last attempt at religion but rather an evening of fun and celebration. The seniors' parents are invited to provide a baby picture of their child. These are collected in advance then a sketch is developed of each senior. The juniors write a short prophecy about each senior and select some song—pop, contemporary, golden oldie, whatever suggests in some way the particular senior. At the banquet, everyone tries to guess the seniors. First the song is played to begin the guessing process. This is followed by a reading of the prophecy. Finally the baby picture is projected. All have found this to be thoroughly enjoyable.

To end the program we read the senior class will, but it is done "ala Howard Hughes." The seniors write their own will but unbeknownst to them the juniors also write one for the seniors. This provides much merriment.—*Timothy Morrison, Auburn, Maine*

Fund raisers

cookie walk

If you're looking for a delicious way to raise funds, you might try a "Cookie Walk." Members of your group bake a great variety of cookies (the more the better), and you raise money by selling cardboard "cookie boxes" to church members and others in the community. The size of the box and price are up to you. We charged

$3.50 per box.

During the "Cookie Walk" those who've bought boxes walk around tables laden with dozens of cookies, choosing their own assortment.

Because this differs from a regular bake sale, be sure to include a short description of what a "Cookie Walk" is all about when you announce the date and time of your event.

And remember that you can sell "cookie boxes" several days or even weeks before the actual affair. In addition to giving you time to reach more people, selling boxes before the date of the "Cookie Walk" will give you an indication of how many cookies your group should bake.— *Vikki Stea, Eugene, Oregon*

windshield wash

A group of Texas high school students recently raised funds for a local project with a "windshield wiper brigade."

Enthusiastic students, armed with clean rags and window cleaner, worked one Saturday afternoon at the parking lot of a large shopping mall. Offering to clean car windows for a 25-cent donation, they

found a surprising response from car owners arriving and departing from the lot. The cleaning process took an average of one minute, and generous tips were offered to the workers to clean the chrome or dashboard. A steady clientele was ensured by shoppers arriving in large numbers throughout the day.

Colorful posters placed at the entrance of the parking lot told of the 25-cent charge, and the project for which the students were raising the funds.

With the decline and expense of full-service gas stations, shoppers were pleased at this low-cost convenience provided by the students.

At the end of an extremely busy day, the group found they had earned twice as much money as anticipated and made plans to work at other large parking lots across the city for future projects.

With little preparation and a small investment in spray window

cleaners, this innovative idea turned into a profitable success.
—*Sharon R. Saine, Austin, Texas*

"free" car wash

We operate a "free" car wash that makes big money.

We do not charge people to wash their cars. Instead, our members solicit sponsors who pledge a certain amount of money for each car washed. Then we wash as many cars as possible in the time we have.

It's important to publicize the car wash in the church and surrounding area so people will bring their cars.

We had a three-hour car wash, washed 100 cars and raised $520. We're planning another one, for which each of our members must have pledges that total $1 per car. This means that $45 per car will be pledged. We should wash about 200 cars in six hours. That's $9000!

We use multiple washing lines, with a work team on each line. We work in two-hour shifts.

We also set up a donation box (just in case). We received an extra $32 from the box during our last wash. Plus, we operate a simultaneous bake sale.

All drivers are asked to sign their name and address on a sheet, so we have proof of the cars washed.—*Jan Hancock, Highland Park United Methodist Church, Dallas, Texas*

truck wash

Our dirtiest (but most memorable and talked about) fund raiser was a truck wash.

We made arrangements with a local trucking firm to wash their big vans for $10 per truck. They provided the buckets, soap, and long brushes, and we provided ten bodies and lots of elbow grease. It was a dirty, wet, and messy job, but we washed ten trucks for a total of $100. We also had a camera handy, and got some great photos!
—*Brian Newcombe, Albany, Oregon*

cafe take-over

We "take over" local restaurants.

We make arrangements with local restaurants to work there on a given Saturday as busboys, waiters and waitresses, cashiers, and hosts and hostesses. The management agrees to pay a percentage of the profits for the day to the group.

Our members participate in a day of training and orientation prior to the work day.

We also do extensive publicity with posters, flyers and announcements in the church paper to encourage people to eat at the restaurant during that day. This is great free publicity for the restaurant.

We have no cost involved. And in addition to making big money, it's a great experience for our group.

For added income, we're planning a car wash simultaneously in the restaurant's parking lot.—*Jan Hancock, Highland Park United Methodist Church, Dallas, Texas*

all night bake sale

Here's a bake sale with a little different twist. Our group made a good profit from an all night baking party.

It is important to make items that you know most people enjoy. We chose chocolate chip and peanut butter cookies, brownies and hot fudge sauce. The kids divided up the church directory, called every member of the church, and asked for orders. From the orders we calculated how much of various ingredients we needed. Because of the size of our grocery order, a local grocer gave us a reduced price. Our church kitchen has four ovens, so it was ideal for the "Great Bake Off."

We met at the church early Friday evening and divided up into various crews: mixers, bakers, packagers. We traded jobs throughout the entire night. We stopped to have breakfast together and then we hit the road to deliver all the goodies.

After the cloud of flour settled, there were those of us who never wanted to see another chocolate chip or peanut butter cookie, but it was a great time. It was a unifying experience to work together all night, and when the last penny was counted we found we had made better than $600. —*Rev. Jim Baar, Grand Rapids, Michigan*

radio day

We have an annual "Radio Day" on one of our local radio stations.

We work out a suitable day with the station management. This year it was February 20, during the station's slow period of the year. We organize a sales committee of youth and adults who call on businesses to encourage them to advertise during Radio Day. Rates were established by the station. Example: five 60-second ads for $25. We split the money 50-50 with the station.

The ads are read live by our members on Radio Day. This becomes somewhat of a riot when they try to "break up" those who are reading. We're very creative in the techniques we use that day. We do skits, choral ads, etc.

Radio Day not only raised $1500 for our group, but it gave our group and church some very positive exposure to the radio audience.—*Larry Bradley, Pine Forest United Methodist Church, Dublin, Georgia*

soup Sunday

Looking for a good winter fund raiser? Try soup.

Our group sponsored a Soup Sunday. It was easy, and it helped our treasury. We enlisted the help of a congregation member who's known for his good Italian cooking. After gathering all the ingredients he requested, we worked one Saturday preparing the soup.

On Soup Sunday we made a special announcement in church. We asked three ladies who were considered the congregation's best cooks to come forward and sample our soup. These "professional tasters" were impressed and helped attract a big crowd for us after the service.

We charged 29 cents for a cup of soup and french bread. But we made it clear that larger donations would be gladly accepted.

Everyone enjoyed the soup. Some people bought quarts of soup to take home ($1.50 per quart). We sold almost all of the 80 quarts that we had prepared. And we made $111.—*Sue Loper, Walnut Creek, California*

buy a mile

This project is a take-off on the old "rising thermometer" idea.

We took a large colored sheet of poster board and sketched a map of our travel route to and from the National Christian Youth Congress. We added up all of our travel expenses and divided by the total number of miles we'd be traveling. After coming up with our cost per mile, we began drawing a red line over our route, showing how far we'd get on the money received thus far.

Church members were given the opportunity over the next few months to help advance us around the route by buying a number of miles. As money was received each week, the line was extended.

This plan had two primary benefits in addition to the money raised. First, it really unified the church family in supporting our youth trip. The whole project was one of cooperation because church contributions were combined with our funds that we raised in other ways. Second, the chart provided a great visual picture of how we all were doing. It became a focal point each Sunday as our members and the congregation came to church.—*Brian Newcombe, North Albany Baptist Church, Albany, Oregon*

flag painters

A group in Decatur, Georgia, raised $100 one Saturday by painting little red mailbox flags.

The members went door to door in their neighborhoods, charging homeowners a quarter to paint the little flags.

Materials required are red enamel paint, some small cups for paint, and paint brushes for each member.—*Brewster McLeod, Cincinnati, Ohio*

fat-a-thon

We've used a fat-a-thon. Both of our ministers were overweight. So we decided to help them lose some pounds and gain some money for our group.

We challenged them to a weight-losing contest. And we solicited pledges for each pound lost.

The contest lasted for several weeks. And when it was over, everyone was a winner. Our senior minister lost 15 pounds, and the associate minister lost 22 pounds. And we collected $381 from our pledges.—*Susan Hughey, Tyler, Texas*

bake auction

Our group sponsors a bake auction.

First we set a theme for the auction. Then our members go to work baking the goodies according to the theme. *Only* the kids are allowed to enter goods. No mom-baked goodies allowed.

Then we set the time for the auction—right after church on Sunday when everyone is hungry. We select an auctioneer who calls the bids just like a regular auction.

Our most recent auction was held by our baseball team. One player baked a cake that looked like a bat and ball. Another baked one that resembled an open Bible. It sold for $40.

Our bake auctions easily raise $200 each time.—*Rev. Foch Fuller, Granada Hills, California*

Bible costume party

We hosted a biblical costume party.

Through our church bulletin, we advertised our upcoming party. We started advertising two months prior, so everyone would have time to make costumes. We set the party for a Saturday night and sold tickets in advance for $1 per person. We sold about 50 tickets.

At the party, we asked each person to get up and tell a short story about the person or thing he or she was portraying.

Our party included many big names from the pages of the Bible—Goliath, Esther, Noah and one little old red-haired lady who dressed up as the burning bush. Our pastor dressed as Moses and I was Samuel.

We had a great time. And we learned something about biblical characters in a really personal way.—*David Silvey, BYF Youth Group, Alexandria, Pennsylvania*

dog wash

A church group in Little Rock, Arkansas, recently raised money for the local Humane Society with a dog wash.

Members charged 2 cents a pound for each dog (and in one case, a skunk!) they washed. Owners brought in their dogs to be weighed on a regular bathroom scale and then carried them over to the wash crews. The dogs were soaped, scrubbed, and then rinsed with a garden hose. A dry job with old rags and a blow dryer, and the job was complete.

The dog wash was held on the church's parking lot on a Saturday. Since the proceeds were to go for a good cause, the newspapers helped to publicize the event. Some dog owners were so pleased with the results that they promised additional donations to the Humane Society.

In a few hours, group members had raised over $100, not including the additional donations.

Supplies: soap, water, a bathroom scale, a garden hose, blow dryers, old rags and brushes, and an energetic crew.—*Sharon Saine, Little Rock, Arkansas*

light bulb sale

Light bulbs make a good fund raiser. Here's how we did it.

First we located a wholesale light bulb dealer in town. You may need to make some phone calls to find a wholesaler. (One company that sells wholesale bulbs for fund raising is United Fund Raisers Co., P.O. Box 894, Dothan, AL 36302, 1-800-633-7557.)

We sold the bulbs for $2.25 instead of the $2.36 that was marked on the packs. We paid $1.16 per pack of four, giving us a profit of $1.09 per pack.

Since our goal was $1,500, our 30 members were each required to sell 50 packs. Members were allowed to keep half the profit on every pack over the first 50 they sold.

The bulb company advised us to buy the bulbs in this ratio: two 60-watt; one 75-watt; and two 100-watt. This turned out to be a good indicator of the way people buy bulbs.

In our group, 13 members sold over the required number of packs. We made our $1,500 goal.

Due to a lack of salesmanship by some members, a number of families are now the proud owners of 30 or so packs of light bulbs. They're stocked for life.—*Ted Johanson, Milwaukee, Wisconsin*

sundae Sunday

Sundae Sunday is a day when our youth put on an ice cream smorgasbord and some kind of entertainment for people in our church.

We buy a large quantity of vanilla ice cream (seven gallons feeds 100 people). We sell the ice cream for 75 cents a dish.

We have a table set up with all kinds of ice cream toppings, so the people can visit this table and create their own sundaes. Toppings include hot fudge, hot butterscotch, hot caramel, strawberries, marshmallow creme, brandied fruit, chopped nuts, sprinkles, granola, coconut and whipped cream. (It is best to have these donated because the expense of buying commercial toppings is prohibitive. We provide some recipes for homemade toppings.)

About 20-25 kids are always involved in this event, either working on the ice cream or on the entertainment. Jobs include scoopers, runners who keep topping supplies filled, table managers who help children serve toppings, people who serve the whipped cream (less waste to have someone serve it), people who take money and tickets, and people who clean up.

The entertainment has been fairly simple. The first year we did the Donna and Murray Show, which featured the talents of our kids. The

youth choir did a concert last year. This year we plan to do a musical with another church in the area.

We have found it helpful to sell tickets in advance, although we usually plan for more people than the tickets we've sold. Some people may buy two dishes of ice cream during the event.

A couple of helpful hints: check with local dairies to see about their bulk pack ice cream prices and/or keep your eyes open for sales at local grocery stores; fondue pots are great for serving hot toppings.
—*UMYF, First United Methodist Church, Cocoa, Florida*

Mother's Day corsage sale

This fund raiser brings a little happiness to mom. Sell Mother's Day corsages. (This would also work for Easter and Christmas.)

Locate a florists' wholesaler or a generous florist who will sell you flowers at cost. Carnations are a good choice for corsages.

Take advance orders. Call every man in your church directory. Put your orders on separate sheets so that each finished corsage can have its own order form attached.

One week in advance, everyone should gather for a training session. Perhaps you have a florist in your church who could teach everyone how to make corsages.

Gather everything you'll need for the corsages—ribbon, wire, pins, etc. These can usually be obtained from the same source as the flowers. Boxes or plastic bags may be used for the finished products.

On the Saturday morning before Mother's Day, pick up your flowers and go to work. Store the finished corsages in a refrigerator.

Inform your customers that they may pick up their corsages on Saturday afternoon. Also set up a delivery service. Charge a nominal additional fee for delivery.

Make some extras to sell Sunday before church.—*Richard G. Steinbrueck, Dunedin, Florida*

bread festival

A "bread festival" mixes fun, fellowship and fund raising.

All members (or their moms) bake three loaves of their favorite kind of bread. Then, after church on Sunday, invite the congregation to the church kitchen or fellowship hall for the bread festival.

Serve free coffee and punch and allow everyone to taste samples

of the different kinds of bread. Then encourage the samplers to buy loaves of their favorite breads. It's great fun, and since everyone likes homemade bread, you should sell out.—*Shane Noel, New London, Iowa*

Christmas crafts day

Our group had a good fund raiser on one of the school holidays a few days before Christmas. It accomplished several things: 1) It gave parents of small children some extra time to do their holiday shopping. 2) It provided a morning of fun and learning for 4- through 9-year olds. 3) It provided a model for younger children of teenagers who are involved in their church. 4) It put everyone in the spirit of Christmas giving. 5) It made a profit of $212.

The project was a Christmas arts and crafts morning. About 25 teenagers helped with it and almost 100 youngsters participated. The members of our youth group purchased supplies (beads, styrofoam, paints, ornament kits, etc.) for the hand-making of Christmas tree ornaments. The young children went to tables, by age, made at least two ornaments and then took them to another table where they were assisted in gift-wrapping them for Mother, Dad, or whomever they liked.

The morning also included Christmas story-telling, carol singing, and refreshments. Tickets for the activity were $3 for the first child in the family, $2 for the second, $1 for the third, and the rest were free.
—*JoAnn Duffy, Orange Park, Florida*

New Year's babysitting service

Looking for a good fund raiser? Need a group activity for New Year's Eve? Combine the two!

Announce in your church and community that your group is offering a super babysitting service for New Year's Eve. Set a price per child, and ask the parents to drop off their children (with sleeping bags) at the church. They may pick them up the following morning.

Plan all kinds of fun stuff for the kids: games, movies, refreshments. When they have thoroughly exhausted your group, tuck them in their sleeping bags. You may want to divide the kids into age groupings.

Serve breakfast for the kids the next morning before the parents come.

This is a fun fund raiser, a good service to parents, and a different way to spend New Year's Eve.

Note

Have you discovered a good youth group idea that's not in this book? Send it to us. GROUP Magazine is always looking for fresh ideas for crowd breakers, games, discussions, worships, service projects and fund raisers. For each of your ideas published in GROUP, you'll receive a check.

Send your ideas to:

"Try This One"
GROUP Magazine
P.O. Box 481
Loveland, CO 80539